THE FREQUENCY
OF WEALTH

BRENTON MIX

ISBN: 978-1-5356-1578-5

Wealth:

1. The state of being rich and affluent.
2. The quality of profuse abundance.

My definition of wealth:

A profuse abundance of health, love, happiness, purpose, vitality, time, and money.

Contents

Introduction

It's been a long journey to get here. I have always wanted to learn the secrets of life, and especially to know the mechanisms for sustained health, wealth, and happiness. For most of my life I believed what everyone seems to believe — that wealth and success come from hard work, persistence, and effort. With that belief I accomplished much. I built several multi-million-dollar businesses, I led companies with thousands of employees, I went from being a poor kid in rural Nebraska to being a multi-millionaire. I enjoyed many long-term relationships, including marriage and children. I was extremely fit and a fairly high-level amateur athlete in a number of different sports. I was also spiritual, thoughtful, kind, and generous. I truly cared about people and gave much of my time and money to various good causes. I had a wealth of friendships and a very good life.

However, about every two or three years, my life would fall apart, businesses on the brink of collapse, relationships pushed to the edge as well. No matter how much I worked and *endeavored* to build a stronger, more secure life, I always found myself engulfed by ever-larger life-tsunamis.

By my thirty-fifth year my once-invincible health had begun to collapse from the burden of the years of stress and I was forced to re-evaluate everything. Through that process I discovered some startling facts. I began to rebuild my life on a new and radical premise — which began to provide powerful, consistent results. After several years of practice and positive results, I began to share what I had discovered with a few other people who sought me out and told me they "wanted what I had." Over the next decade, I worked with several dozen people, helping them implement the ideas that I wish to share with you here in this book. I worked with each person for about a year and we usually met once each week during that time. The information was transformational for all of the individuals I worked with, without exception, and they each experienced dramatic improvements in health, happiness, relationship satisfaction and, of course, wealth.

While I feel blessed to have unlocked the wisdom contained in this book and honored to have been able to share it with the people I've worked with, I have been *very* reluctant to write this book. I feared that my message would look, at first glance, like another "self-help" or "get rich" book — and thus the depth of the message would be missed.

As I've previously mentioned, the success I've had helping people transform their lives has come from working directly with them. I am excited to discover how effectively this information can be transmitted through written form. I have concluded that the need for this wisdom greatly outweighs my own resistance — for far too many people are suffering greatly in their lives. Lives that could otherwise be full of purpose, vitality, freedom, satisfaction, and joy. Thus, I have decided that if by writing this book I can help to alleviate suffering and help individuals experience the profound sense of joy and freedom that is their natural birthright, then it is my duty to endeavor to at least try and share my story and experience with you.

Finally, this book is meant to get you started. My goal is to reveal the laws and processes by which your *reality* is being created, so that you can more effectively manifest the things you want and need, and so that you may more quickly live the life you know you were meant to live. So, on that note, let us begin:

"For, behold, the kingdom of God is within you."
Luke 17:21

Wealth Has a Frequency

THE PREMISES OF THIS BOOK are:

- You are a vibrational being.
- You live in a vibrational universe.
- Your senses (eyes, ears, nose, etc.) transmit these vibrations to your brain.
- Your brain takes these vibrations and creates the 3D world you experience.
- The world you experience is an exact frequency match to the inner vibrational signal you emit.
- Your emotions are designed to tell you what frequency you are emitting.
- You have a natural, divine right to wealth, health, and happiness.
- Health, wealth, abundance, and happiness are natural states and exist on the high end of the frequency spectrum.
- You create your life from the inside out.
- Your emotions tell you the frequency you are currently on.

- You have the ability to tune your emotions to the life you want to experience.
- You reap what you sow. If you sow seeds of stress, struggle, and unhappiness, you will reap a harvest — a life — that matches those frequencies. If you sow seeds of peace, joy, happiness, and wellbeing, you will reap a harvest of the same.
- Wealth is a far more powerful reality than poverty, just as abundance is more real than lack, and health more real than disease.
- True wealth appears once you release chronic resistance and consistently feel good.

Radio Dial of Wealth

AN EFFECTIVE METAPHOR FOR HOW to manifest wealth is a car radio.

When you listen to the radio, you tune your radio dial to the station you want to listen to. You can only listen to one station at a time. THE STATIONS ARE ALREADY STREAMING MUSIC ALL OF THE TIME. But you can only "experience" the music from the station that you are tuned to.

- You don't create, make an effort for, struggle for, or otherwise "make" the music — you simply tune to the frequency of the radio station playing the music you want to listen to. Wealth works exactly the same way. You tune to its frequency, and it comes flooding in.
- There are innumerable stations on the human radio dial, and your inner frequency — emotional set-point — determines which one you receive/ experience.

- There is a spectrum of radio "stations," from total lack on one end, to profuse abundance on the other, and everything in between.
- Happy people meet happy circumstances; unhappy people find the world to be an unhappy place. Two people can be sitting next to each other, and one of them can be experiencing a miserable world while the other experiences a happy world full of wonders.
- Your own observation will prove this truth to you.
- To change your life, you must change your average emitted frequency — your emotional set-point.

Unfortunately, whether they realize it or not, most people believe the opposite is true. They believe "I'm unhappy now, and if I change my circumstances, then I'll be happy." So we chase after more money, a different job, a different place to live, a different body to live in, a new relationship, all the while emitting the same frequencies that manifested the life we are living in the first place. Thus, "different places, different faces," but life remains largely the same.

Many of us go further: we work harder, suffer more, endeavor more, in order to change our "external" life. However, if our internal vibration doesn't change, nothing will change for long. This is why diets, savings plans, new relationships, etc., fail so often. Unless we change the inside, the outside will revert back. However, if the diet or savings plan, or new job or relationship, helps to change our internal frequencies (thoughts and beliefs), then we will see lasting results.

The simplest, most direct, and lasting results come from taking control of your "tuner" and changing your frequency directly.

If you want *health, wealth, and happiness*, you must tune to those stations and the music will automatically appear.

The main purpose of this book is to teach you how you can take control of your emotional frequency and use that control to tune into the frequencies you want, such as wealth, so that you begin to live the life you were meant to live.

Emotional Guidance System

IT IS TRUE THAT YOUR thoughts create your life. And by changing/improving your thoughts, you change/improve your life. For many of us, the difficulty lies in knowing which thoughts to change and how to change them.

Thankfully, we've been given a powerful mechanism to tell us exactly which thoughts are causing the problems in our life and holding us back from our health, wealth, and happiness. This mechanism is your emotions. The term I prefer is *Emotional Guidance System*. Because that's exactly what it is. Like a compass, or a navigation system in your car or smart-phone, your emotional guidance system provides powerful feedback on the thoughts and beliefs that are keeping you from wealth.

This is similar to the pain system in your body. There are roughly 37 trillion cells in the human body, over 600 muscles, 206 bones, 12 organ systems, etc. Your autonomic system is managing a complex universe of activity. So, what do you, your "conscious self," have to pay attention to? It would be impossible to try and consciously manage the trillions of activities that are happening each day. So, you have a powerful, elegant system called pain. It's very effective, wouldn't you say? Pain in your body gives you quick information, getting your attention so that you can change something you or your body are doing. And like emotions, there are all kinds of gradations of sensations in the body — from the warm, pleasant feeling of a hot shower to the "good" pain of exercising the body to the very sharp pain when we cut our finger or bump our head.

Emotions are very similar. Thought-form is a complex system of creation in this dimension. You have roughly 50,000 thoughts per day. Which ones are holding you back? It's nearly impossible to observe, manage, and change thousands and thousands of thoughts each day.

Mercifully, we don't have to. Our emotional guidance system comes to the rescue. This elegant system gives us real-time, actionable information on the world we are creating through our thoughts. All emotions are helpful messengers attempting to tell us important information. And if we ignore them, they get louder and louder — just like pain in the body.

Tuning Process

ONCE YOU BEGIN TO UNDERSTAND the vibrational basis of this universe — the fact that your life is created through thought-form, that your emotions tell you the vibrational frequencies that you are emitting, and that your outer life reflects and matches those frequencies — then learning how to improve your vibrational output becomes paramount. I call this process of vibrational improvement and control the Tuning Process.

The Tuning Process that I employ is a five-point method:

1. Emotional Awareness
2. Truth Immersion
3. Releasing Resistance
4. Expanding Wellbeing
5. Leaning Into Joy

These five aspects are not chronological — they do not need to be done in order. However, all five need to be utilized — in one way or another — for maximum acceleration into your best life.

Again, what we are accomplishing here is a dramatic improvement in your overall vibrational set-point. And, effectively employed, these five steps will make a dramatic impact.

Emotional Awareness

Your ***vibrational set-point*** is known to you by the way you feel. It is vital that you are aware of how you feel to improve the overall frequencies (via thought-form) that you emit. Fundamentally, just knowing the basic function of your emotions — to get your attention regarding your thoughts — will help develop awareness. Many of us have suppressed, ignored, or misunderstood our emotions for much of our lives. So it's going to take some time for the "noise" to subside and to begin to hear the clear and distinct "signals" your emotional guidance system is giving you.

However, just understanding the basic role of emotions will be a powerful beginning. It's enough of a start to realize the "warmer/colder" emotional information we are receiving is guiding us to the life and wealth we desire.

For instance, when you think of money, do you feel good or stressed? It's enough of a beginning to start to realize that when you think about certain subjects/things/people, you do have habituated thought patterns and those patterns produce an emotional response from your guidance system.

As you develop an awareness of the emotional responses you have to your habituated thoughts, you will begin to notice that some subjects, when you think about them, feel better than others. Over time you will begin to realize that you have a great degree of control over what you think and, therefore, how you feel. Most of us have never actually taken control of our thought-life. Thoughts, thought patterns, and most especially our emotional lives are something that happen to us, not something we believe we have control over. So: begin to notice your feeling response to various subjects you are thinking about.

Here is a very important question: Are there any areas of your life that, when you think about them, make you feel good? Can you narrow it down to something small, like the laughter of your children, your cat purring, your dog wagging its tail, the sun shining in your face, a cool ocean breeze? Maybe a favorite memory of your best vacation, a time in life when you were particularly happy — laughing with friends or holding your newborn baby. As you take time to think about particular thoughts that bring relief, joy, a smile to your face, you will begin to know that you CAN think thoughts that feel better, thoughts that improve your emotional/vibrational set-point.

You're going to start to work thought-muscles you may have never really used before — the muscles that allow you to use your willpower and choose to think better-feeling thoughts and deny thoughts/subjects that make you feel terrible. Again, it's not that "bad" feelings are bad, any more than pain in the body is bad. Pain is a vital, precious feedback system telling you to pay attention to something important and to possibly change course. Negative emotions are similar. They are delivering vital, precious information regarding thoughts that are holding back your best life.

Truth Immersion

The majority of the work I do with people is in this step. There is something very powerful, very transformative that happens when we learn about how it all works. I spend a lot of time educating people about, reminding them of, and reinforcing these basic tenets:

- You are a vibrational being, living in a vibrational universe.
- Wealth is a frequency that is streaming all of the time.

- In fact, wealth, health, peace, and harmony are all far more real and abundant than lack, sickness, misery, and discord.
- When you attune to these frequencies of reality, they appear in your experience.
- Your emotions tell you the frequency you are emitting *and* receiving.
- The better you feel, the better your life gets; not the other way around.
- You can control your emotional/vibrational set-point by using your **willpower** to choose better-feeling thoughts and focusing your attention on thoughts and subjects that uplift, while denying and distracting yourself from thoughts and subjects that pull you down.
- You are meant to live a joyful, abundant, fulfilling life, and that is far more natural to your being than a stressful, scarcity-based, unfulfilling life.
- The best way to help/serve others is to live a joyful life.

I find that these and other truths need to be reinforced daily. Once you learn you can significantly influence the vibration you emit, and you learn some basic ways to do it (which I will provide in the next three steps), then it really is about reminding yourself of what IS TRUE. I try and consume nutritious mind-food (Truth) every day, many times a day. I use YouTube, podcasts, books, books on tape, etc., to feed my mind with the Truth daily. It doesn't take much — 10 or 15 minutes of ingesting Truth throughout my day is enough to keep my vibration stabilized and tuned to the high frequencies I want.

I give my clients the list of sources I use — daily meditations, quotes, authors, speakers, books that speak the Truth. And here's where you have to be careful. My experience is that there are a few, but not many, who understand the Truth. Most have a bit of the truth, and then add a bunch of non-truths, and thus the vibrational waters get muddied.

I also find that my clients benefit significantly from my "knowing" of these truths and use our sessions to re-up/boost their vibration.

The great news is that these truths are simply a way of describing the cause and effect of how consciousness (you) creates in this dimension. Once you have a basic understanding of the concepts, your own life — past, present, and future — will prove the merit of it.

It seems to me that the Truth is just a lot of information that seems "too good to be true." So good, in fact, that at first, it's hard to believe. Part of that good news is that you don't have to take my word for any of this; once you get a basic understanding of the concepts, you can prove it to yourself. You can look back over your life and see the correlation between thoughts, feelings, and the life that results from them. Like gravity, this law of vibration is happening all the time, silently, pervasively, whether you believe it or not. You can also look at people around you and see the law working in their lives.

Your emotional life = your life.

When you FEEL good, life IS good. When you feel bad emotionally, it is very difficult to see and experience an abundant life. So, if feeling good means that you are creating the life you want, then everything becomes about finding ways to feel better emotionally. And when you think about it, everything you desire — health, wealth, love — you desire because you think you will feel better in the having of it. The Truth is, if you **FEEL** better **FIRST**, you will then ultimately get everything you desire.

The art of feeling good drives everything. It really does.

Releasing Resistance

When I speak of resistance, I mean resistant thoughts. Your vibrational set-point is naturally high. As with the body, it is far more natural for you to be vibrationally healthy than to be diseased. It's like pulling a cork under water: your habituated thoughts of lack, poverty, guilt, shame, unworthiness, fear, stress, or blame have pulled your "vibrational" cork down into dark waters where all the dark thoughts live. So how do we make your vibrational cork float on the water and bask in the sunlight of wealth, health, and happiness? By letting go of resistance.

What does a cork do in water? It floats. That's what it does. **That's its nature.**

What does your vibration naturally do? It rises. It floats. It attunes to health, wealth, and happiness. That's what it does. That's its nature.

I think it's fantastic news that we do not actually need to *endeavor and strain* and work to push, push, push our vibrations up a long, arduous hill to get to the promised land. In fact, for many of us, our effort and struggle and hard, hard work has actually been keeping us poor.

We strain and struggle and stress to achieve wealth, but all the while we are actually lowering our vibration. And therefore, even if we are making lots of money, or "achieving" at a high level, we are never actually wealthy. It's costing us our health, our marriages, our relationships with our family and children, and we have no peace. And for the record, you cannot be wealthy without peace.

So how do we "let go" of resistance? It's actually pretty easy, although most of us will struggle at first. Remember, you've had a lifetime of developing some pretty resistant thought patterns and beliefs; it can take a little bit of time and practice to move in a new direction.

Fundamentally, it's very simple: <u>Stop thinking thoughts that lower your vibration (make you feel worse) and replace them with thoughts that elevate your vibration (uplift you emotionally).</u>

Here are some effective ways to do just that:

Strategic Distraction. Because health, wealth, and abundance is a more substantial reality than poverty and sickness, you don't need to be thinking abundance/ wealth to experience wealth. However, you cannot be focused on its opposite and experience the thing you want. It's like being in a room filled with gold but having your eyes closed. You simply need to open your eyes.

You are emitting one frequency, one signal, at a time. Everything you want, wealth, health, and happiness, already exists at the higher end of the frequency chart (see "Radio Dial of Wealth"). Emit any frequency at that end and you will begin to experience all forms of wealth — again, provided you do not immediately decide to focus on the opposite. This was my primary issue. I had health, wealth of friends and relationships, abundance of almost every kind, but all I could see was the lack and absence of money. My "eyes" were closed — and I was cut off from the effortless flow. Trapped in the cycle of effort and struggle.

And it's so obvious. People who don't worry about money do not have money problems. People who worry about money have money problems. The same is true for all subjects — health, love, relationships, etc.

Unfortunately for me, I had what seemed like an impervious poverty consciousness. I just couldn't shake it. No matter how hard I tried. Every time I thought about money, I was actually <u>thinking about the lack of money</u>. So it was great news when I learned I didn't have to think about an abundance of money to materialize an abundance of money — I just had to stop myself from thinking about its absence. Actually, I didn't stop (you don't have to stop completely); I just stopped doing it ALL THE TIME. And I did it through the technique of distraction.

Here's how it works: As often as you can, find activities that hold your attention so much that you forget to think your normal thoughts of stress and worry (or whatever the negative-feeling thoughts are that are holding you back). I built my entire day around this single principle. And it worked like a charm.

For me it was exercise, mixed martial arts, mentoring, coffee with friends, naps, and comedy movies. Anything that got me to temporarily forget to worry about money.

I would wake up in the morning and immediately start freaking out about payroll, bills, the IRS, etc. So the first thing I did was a 5:00 a.m. CrossFit class. I was barely even awake. It was important for me to be around other energetic people to really distract me. If I just went to the weight room by myself, I would worry, worry, worry. So I needed something more dramatic to get my attention.

After CrossFit I would feel pretty good for about two hours. So, with my vibration strong, I would work for a while — meetings, phone calls. By 9:00 a.m. it was starting to fall again, so I would go to my MMA gym and spar — kickboxing and/or grappling. I was an extreme case — no one else I've worked with needed to go to such lengths. However, I can promise you this: you cannot worry about money while you're getting punched in the face.

Sparring would set me up for my afternoon, vibrationally speaking. After work I would come home, spend time with my family, eat dinner, and then meet up with a friend or do some service work (mentoring), which would completely distract my mind until evening. Before I went to sleep, I would watch a comedy.

I did that each day, or some variation of that, for two years. And I watched my life transform around me. All forms of abundance and wealth began to appear.

Again, the principle is that you send one frequency at a time. Find the subject and/or activities that feel good while you're doing them, and your entire life will respond to that higher vibration.

Meditation. I didn't utilize conscious meditation until I learned about the vibrational cause and effect of how wealth is created/experienced. Then I really got on board with it because I saw its tremendous vibrational value. For me the only value of meditation is to improve my vibration — and that's exclusively how I employ it.

When I feel low, I use a 15-minute breathing meditation to focus/distract my mind, which allows my vibrational "cork" to float. When I'm feeling good, I utilize the breathing meditation, followed by a body-scan/sensory-scan meditation to expand my "wellbeing muscles" (we'll address this in the "Expanding Wellbeing" section), again with the purpose of increasing my vibration and vibrational set-point.

Finally, anytime I notice that I'm stressed out or unnecessarily holding tension in my body, I will use a short 30-second to two-minute "releasing" meditation that involves breath-work and conscious relaxing. I'll do this anywhere — in the car, at work, before a meeting, after receiving "bad" news, at home with my kids; anywhere.

There are hundreds of books on this subject that can be a great resource for learning meditation techniques; here I'm going to briefly cover two types of meditation — the 10-to-15-minute breathing meditation and the 30-second relaxing meditation.

Daily Breathing Meditation. Here's what I do: I lie down in bed or sit in a comfortable chair. I get as absolutely comfortable as I can. I then start to breathe deeply in and out. I count to six or eight while I'm breathing in, and I count to four or six when I'm breathing out. I never hold my breath at the "top" or "bottom" of the breath. It's meant to be deep and natural. The purpose of the counting is to focus my mind on counting and breathing. During the 10 to 15 minutes I am constantly redirecting my thoughts back to my breathing and counting. My mind wants to wander, which is totally fine and natural, but I gently and continually redirect it back to counting and breathing. One…two…three…four…five…six (breathing in through the nose) … One…two…three…four…five (breathing out through the mouth). In…and out…

It can take a while to get the hang of it, but once you do, it's powerful. I do this at least five days a week. It is possibly the most important thing I do to "create" wealth.

After spending so many years in stressful action-effort, attempting to force my achievement of goals and ambitions, I'm still stunned at how much more effective and powerful 15 minutes of conscious-breathing meditation is to affect those same goals and ambitions. For those of us stuck in the "effort-matrix," it's counter-logical. Once you grasp the truth of the vibrational world and how thought-form creates it, it becomes very obviously effective.

Short, 30-second meditation. I use this when I'm getting agitated, stressed, or worried and I don't have time for the longer breathing meditation, such as when I'm driving or at the office, etc. Similarly to the breathing meditation, I start breathing deeply — in through the nose, out through the mouth, counting as I do it (to focus my mind away from lower-vibrating thoughts), and I then focus on releasing tension in my body, starting with my solar plexus (basically my stomach) and moving quickly to other muscles/areas of my body, such as my face/brow, jaw, hands, arms, shoulders, back, legs, etc. Just a quick body scan to release tension. I'm always surprised at how much tension I'm holding without realizing it in those situations. It's a quick way to reverse course and start vibing up. I usually end with a quick affirmation/prayer that sets my attention and intention on the Truth.

Affirmation. This can be tricky. I spent a lot of time in my twenties attempting to use positive affirmations and failing miserably. This was primarily because I did not yet know the law of vibration. The whole, entire point of any of these tools and techniques, including affirmations, is to RAISE your vibration and, therefore, how you feel. If that's not happening, or worse, if it's actually lowering your vibration, stop. I spent years saying words I wanted to believe, but it was actually reminding me of the absence of all of these things (safety, security, health, wealth, etc.) and therefore had no real positive effect. So now I only use affirmations when they either give me relief or help me feel better. When they can accomplish either of those two things, I use them.

Another benefit of using an affirmation is that you can use it repetitively, like a mantra. This, like the breathing meditation, helps to focus my mind on something good, and pulls my focus away from lower-vibrating thoughts.

There are too many great affirmations to list, but I will give you the one I've used most:

"All is well. Everything is working out for my highest good. Out of this situation, only good will come. I am safe."

This affirmation is from Louise Hay. She has hundreds of powerful statements just like this one. The key for me on this affirmation is that I believe it completely. I do believe it. So, in combination with my other releasing techniques, I like to say this out loud, when I'm alone in my car, and repeat it several times. I use it when I'm "buying the lie" that everything is about to fall apart.

What is important when using a mantra is that it makes you feel better, or, at the very least, gives you some relief. Use whatever words or thoughts or processes accomplish that single goal.

Expanding Wellbeing

This is a bit of a misnomer. We don't really "expand" wellbeing; what we do is expand our ability to <u>notice</u> and <u>appreciate</u> the vast, powerful ever-presence of wellbeing. Wellbeing, harmony, balance, homeostasis; these are interchangeable words.

The good news is that wellbeing is fundamental to our beingness. It's our natural state. This is where we live, if not actively held down with negative thoughts.

When I first started it took me a long time to get to wellbeing, to actually just feel stable and good. Maybe a better way of describing "wellbeing" is the absence of stress, worry, guilt, shame — any negative thought. Let me reinforce the good news that we don't have to push, push, push our vibration up a hill and into wellbeing; it's really about temporarily letting go of negative thoughts and beliefs. Again, like a cork that will automatically float to the surface, your vibration will automatically "float" up to wellbeing, if you stop holding it down with negative thoughts.

For a long time, I couldn't fight the negative thoughts in my mind. The more I tried to "let go" of stress and worry, the more I stressed and worried. This is why distraction is so fantastic. I have yet to work with someone who cannot find several activities that distract the mind enough to temporarily move your core vibration up to wellbeing. It's a wonderful trick.

Catch-Myself-Happy Game. Here's a fun game to play. See how many times each day you can catch yourself being happy. What is happy? **Happy is the absence of worry, stress, fear, hate, blame, resentment, guilt — anything negative.** It's not necessarily the presence of joy or excitement (although it can certainly include those), but rather simply the absence of bad. There was so much "noise" in my head when I began this journey that I really didn't know what happy was, or, more specifically, what it felt like. So, I developed an indirect method of identification — Time. Whenever I lost track of time, I concluded that I was probably happy.

At first, this might only be for seconds at a time. During a workout, or laughing with a friend, or doing service work, or cleaning the house. I began to notice

27

that, at times, I was forgetting to worry. And then it started to grow. I <u>noticed</u> that AFTER working out, or cleaning the kitchen, or laughing with a friend, that wellbeing hung around for a few minutes. I started to look for things that distracted my mind long enough for my cork to automatically float. I found that cleaning a small part of my house every morning felt good; I felt accomplished, for about 10 minutes. I would go to lunch with a friend or business associate and I would actually ***ENJOY*** myself — and, most importantly, I NOTICED that I was enjoying it. That was the key.

Turns out this was happening all through the day. I had been blind to the fact that there were bits and pieces of my day where I was actually happy.

I started to learn how to take control of my attention, and, bit by bit, focus my attention on the things that served me — and served my vibration. After months and months of this, I started to realize that I had access to great joy and happiness in my life.

Wellbeing Meditation. Somewhere in the middle of this, after maybe around six months of working to notice wellbeing, I started employing a Wellbeing Meditation. I absolutely love this one. This is a 10-to-15-minute breathing meditation where the sole objective is to consciously expand your ability to feel good. Generally speaking, this should only be used at the time of day you feel best, or when you already feel really good. It's similar to the *Releasing Resistance Meditation.*

How to Do It. Find a very comfortable place to sit, or, preferably, lie down. Begin to breathe deeply through your nose, and out through your mouth. Count to six or eight on the way in, and four to six on the way out. Don't hold your breath at the top or bottom of the inhale/ exhale. While you're doing this, and because you already feel good, begin to notice how good it feels to feel good.

Notice how good your body feels resting in a wonderful bed. You have 37 trillion cells in your body, working perfectly to support your health. Notice again just how good it feels to feel good. The absence of any pain or discomfort. Slowly use your mind to scan your body, from the hair on your head to the tip of your toes, and how each of these beautiful, elegant systems is working perfectly and harmoniously at this very moment. Feel how good it feels to feel good.

Indulge in Nature. Nature can be a powerful place to raise your vibration and expand wellbeing. It's a very effective place to do the Wellbeing Meditation — while walking in a forest, through a field, on a mountain trail, or by the ocean. Just sitting and listening to the wind blow through the trees, feeling the sun on your face, witnessing the glory of nature.

To improve our vibrational set-point, and thereby experience the life and wealth we wish to, it's critical that we raise the floor on our vibration. Anchoring into wellbeing is a vital part of this.

After months of releasing resistance and expanding your awareness of the overwhelming presence of wellbeing, you will begin to change your vibrational home base from stress and worry to something far more powerful — peace.

Leaning Into Joy

Joy is the real currency of life. It is, in fact, life itself.

The last step in this process is to start doing more of the things you actually enjoy. This may seem easy, but for most of us, it isn't easy at all. We've spent most of our lives learning how to suffer — to put others' needs and wants (our children, family, employer, spouse) ahead of our own. So it can take a little time to get the hang of this step.

The principle here is that is must affect your vibration — you must *feel* it. Through this five-part Tuning Process you will begin to become aware of vibrational differences of thoughts and activities. You will start to see that some things feel better than others. And this is very important:

you may think you enjoy something that you actually don't.

Again, what you say doesn't matter. Your life is determined by the vibration you emit. If you say you enjoy golf when actually you're pretty miserable throughout the round, you need to become aware of that. That vibrational signal of misery is going to tune you into other experiences that are miserable.

For now, let's start as small as we can. Make a list of small things that you really enjoy and that you have immediate access to, such as:

- a hot shower or bath
- petting your cat or walking your dog
- a walk around the neighborhood on a nice day
- a fresh-brewed cup of coffee or tea
- a nap
- a cool pillow
- relaxing in your favorite chair
- talking to a friend
- a quiet meal

It's important that you find daily thoughts and activities that you truly enjoy. It's your mission in this step to **stretch your joy-muscles**. You must recapture your ability to enjoy life. And enjoying life begins with the ability to start enjoying moments. You must become aware of your ability to experience joy and your ability to direct yourself toward things that you like thinking about and doing.

Life is made up of a series of moments. You build the life you've always wanted one moment of joy at a time. As you move toward more and more things that "light you up," over time your life will begin to shift.

This is the life of wealth and abundance — living a joyful life. Through joy, you will find your passion for life, life will have great meaning, you will perform at your highest ability, and the people you love most will benefit most.

The Joy of Living

THE GREATEST GIFT, AND POSSIBLY the only gift, you can give this world is the Spirit of You. Once you begin to live a life 1) largely free of resistant thought and 2) where you engage thoughts and activities that are joyful, you will begin to feel a true freedom and a love of being alive right here, right now. This begins the journey of self-expression. Letting Spirit, Energy, and Vitality pour through you to the great benefit of yourself and others.

When we release condemnation, blame, guilt, and all other resistant thought, *Spirit* awakens within us and a great desire to express Life becomes operative. No longer living stressed-out, depressed, suppressed lives, now we are truly full of Life itself. Health, wealth, love, and happiness are felt within and without. We feel youthful again and excited about life.

This is not a static state, for life is not static. It comes and goes, but it is always available to us as we take control of our thoughts and vibration. Now, our starting point and home base is peace and wellbeing. It becomes second nature and effortless. We move from peace to joy and back again throughout the day. Of course, there are moments of stress, fear, pain, but they are moments and we easily recover from them. In fact, we begin to see the richness of all thoughts and feeling, even the less comfortable ones, now that they no longer control us. Like the spices we use when cooking, a few discomforting feelings in the day can add flavor and are an important part of the joy of the journey. We no longer fear depression or pain, as we know we have the power to regain our peaceful/joyful vibration.

The Frequency of Wealth

CALMNESS, PEACE, EMPOWERMENT, HAPPINESS, JOY, excitement, light-heartedness, laughter, smiles, being in love, satisfaction, relief, feeling thrilled — these are the many frequencies of wealth. If you want to experience more money, health, and vitality than you dreamed possible, then you must enter the emotional state of being where wealth resides in terrific abundance.

We create our life from the inside out. Our emotions tell us the kind of life we are creating. If we are full of strife and bitterness on the inside, our outer life will reflect it. If we constantly stress over life, we will continue to create a life to stress about. Conversely, when we feel good — happy, excited, joyful, peaceful — our outer life will reflect a life of peace, power, and joy.

As we begin to understand how wealth is created (from our thoughts and feelings), and as we understand the powerful role our emotions play, we will see the tremendous value in feeling as good as possible as often as possible.

As you begin to feel better, you will shift your vibrational set-point. As that shifts "upward," as you no longer hold your "cork" under water as often as you did, your life will begin to change for the better.

As you begin to consistently feel better, you will begin to tune into the frequencies of wealth. Over time you will experience more health, more vit ality, a new awakening to the vast abundance that is always available. Joy, health, wealth, love, vitality — these streams of consciousness — these worlds of abundance — are here, all around us. They are here for you to access, like radio stations.

True wealth includes health, happiness, satisfying relationships, joy, peace, and an abundance of money. When you gain control of your emotional life, you gain true wealth. As you learn to achieve these emotional set-points more and more, you will begin to witness a transformation in the outer world of your life.

Your Journey Begins

OKAY, SO THIS BRINGS US to the end of Book One in the *Keys to the Kingdom* series. I trust that I've impressed upon you how your world is created from the inside out — and the critical role your emotions play in shaping that world. Of all the insights I can share, these are most important in creating wealth. Additionally, I've given you the tools to help improve your vibrational set-point, so that you can accelerate the flow of the *wealth, health, and abundance* of every kind into your life.

Now that we've made a beginning, additional books in this series will delve deeper, providing additional information, tools, techniques, and secrets on the nature of reality, consciousness, and how to thrive in this higher dimension.

Blessings to you on your journey, may your Spirit shine brightly in the world, and may you enjoy more of the freedom and abundance that is waiting to flow to you.